HOW TO PARTNER WITH GIRL SCOUT SENIORS ON

GIRLtopia

IT'S YOUR WORLD—CHANGE IT! A LEADERSHIP JOURNEY

Girl Scouts of the USA

CHAIR, NATIONAL BOARD OF DIRECTORS	CHIEF EXECUTIVE OFFICER	EXECUTIVE VICE PRESIDENT, MISSION TO MARKET	VICE PRESIDENT, PROGRAM DEVELOPMENT
Patricia Diaz Dennis	Kathy Cloninger	Norma I. Barquet	Eileen Doyle

WRITERS: Stefanie Glick, Monica Shah

CONTRIBUTORS: Kate Gottlieb, Toi James, Maja Ninkovic

DESIGNED BY Parham Santana

First published in 2008 by Girl Scouts of the USA
420 Fifth Avenue, New York, NY 10018-2798
www.girlscouts.org

ISBN: 978-0-88441-718-7

Printed in Italy

3 4 5 6 7 8 9/16 15 14 13 12 11 10 09 08

Page 16: Photo by Matthew Pennington, Dhahran, Saudi Arabia.

Tips for Talking About Values, page 38, adapted from *Life Planning Education*, Advocates for Youth,
Washington, D.C., www.advocatesforyouth.org

CONTENTS

GETTING TO GIRLtopia 5

Toward the Senior Visionary Award 6

Take Action Planning Chart 8

Scheduling the Journey 10

Sample Sessions at a Glance 12

Choice: It's All Up to the Girls 14

Family, Friends, and an Ever-Growing Circle 15

YOU AND YOUR CREW OF GIRL SCOUT SENIORS 17

Understanding Senior-Age Girls 18

What + How: Creating a Quality Experience 20

Girl Scout Ceremonies and Traditions 22

Health, Safety, and Well-Being 24

Understanding the Journey's Leadership Benefits 26

Your Perspective on Leadership 28

THE JOURNEY'S 8 SAMPLE SESSIONS 33

"**Teen girls . . . are invincible** and ready to try anything. You can't give them any problem that as a group they can't figure out . . . . By giving them the tools they need to reach out and shape their environment, community, and world, I am helping make the next generation of outstanding women ready to take on the world."

—Sam Johnson, Girl Scout volunteer and alumna, Bowie, Maryland

GETTING TO GIRLtopia

Imagine if every girl in the world could attend school, pursue her passions, and choose the career and family life she wanted. Imagine a world in which girls could influence policies that really matter—education, health care, housing, employment.

RIGHT NOW, THIS ISN'T THE CASE.
Consider these statistics:

Half the women in the world above age 15 cannot read or write.[1]

Worldwide, 62 million girls are not attending primary school.[2]

Violence causes more death and disability worldwide among women age 15–44 than war, cancer, malaria, or traffic accidents.[3]

This is how Girl Scout Seniors are introduced to GIRLtopia, a leadership journey that invites them to consider the reality of life for girls throughout the world. As girls take in this reality, they are invited to envision an ideal world—a society that consistently respects their needs, values, and interests.

Through team discussions and reflective experiences, you will guide the Seniors as they act as visionaries who can foresee a GIRLtopia. As the journey progresses, they will create a work of art to represent their ideal vision and then engage in a Take Action Project to move the real world one step closer to their ideal.

[1] Women's Learning Partnership/www.womankind.org.uk
[2] *Because I Am a Girl: The State of the World's Girls 2007* (Plan International)
[3] Directorate of Public Health, UK, via www.womankind.org.uk

Toward the Senior Visionary Award

Sharing the GIRLtopia art projects can be simple, even just showing them to friends and family. Or it can be more elaborate: hosting an exhibit night, creating an online gallery, or hanging a display at a local library. Poetry might be published in a school or local paper or literary magazine, shared via e-mail, or read at a "poetry night." What matters most is that the girls consider, express, and then convey their vision to others.

GREAT IDEAS FOR "GUIDE ITS"

The sample sessions in this guide also suggest "Guide Its" girls might enjoy, and the "Think About It, Talk About Its" throughout their book might generate some great girl-led discussions.

While journeying toward GIRLtopia, girls have the option of earning a major award—the Senior Visionary Award. The Senior Visionary Award is an important step on the Girl Scout leadership ladder; it signifies that girls have a firm leadership foundation. They understand themselves, are able to make ethical decisions, build teams, care about others, envision change, and take action toward it.

To earn the Visionary Award, Seniors will complete three steps, which they can accomplish—as a team or on their own—one by one or simultaneously:

1. Create It: *Create a unique vision and artistic representation of an ideal world, and then share it with others.*

Some girls love art, some don't. On this journey, they can choose a simple yet thoughtful way to represent their vision or they can go all out on an artistic adventure. For example, girls might write a group poem that reflects their ideal community or they might compile favorite songs that address the possibility of a better world. They could make a video of girls talking about how society needs to improve or they could create and perform a short play on the subject. Girls can use any medium they want—photography, painting, collage, written or spoken word, quilting—the choice is all theirs!

2. Guide It: *Guide a mini-discussion or group activity that engages other girls in thinking about visionary leadership.*

This step builds on the leadership topics presented throughout the girls' book, which range from making ethical decisions to creating a Girls' Bill of Rights.

Have the girls divvy up the topics that interest them—or come up with their own—and then take turns offering mini-workshops or discussion sessions for one another or other girls, older or younger, over the course of the journey. For example, a girl might create a teamwork activity that pools the group's talents in preparation for the Take Action Project. Or some girls might want to invite local women leaders to discuss ethical decisions they've had to make, building on the case scenarios presented in the journey. The girls could then follow up by leading a group discussion or interview.

3. Change It: *Do a Take Action Project that moves the world (or a community) one step closer to ideal.*

Girl Scouting unites girls in a global sisterhood, so girls may use their Take Action Project to think globally, but act locally—or think locally and then reach out globally. Even as they concentrate on "girl issues" (page 9 in the girls' book details the state of girls and women in the world today), they'll likely see a broader impact on their whole community.

Most important, girls will experience the 12 stages of taking action, as listed in the Take Action Planning Chart on page 80 of their book and pages 8–9 of this guide. These stages aid girls in developing a process for analyzing issues, getting input from others, assessing their resources (including time) realistically, considering the greatest impact they can have based on their resources, and then planning and acting accordingly.

GOOD TAKE ACTION PROJECTS: CRITICAL THINKING MORE IMPORTANT THAN PROJECT "SIZE"

The time girls spend on their Take Action Project is less important than their having a meaningful opportunity to progress through the stages of identifying, planning, and doing a project. So make use of the coaching steps spelled out in the Take Action Planning Chart on the next pages. The learning that takes place along the way is what will benefit girls now and all their lives. A simpler version of this chart is on page 80 of the girls' book.

THE HOW AND WHY OF "CHANGE IT"

As girls begin to plan their Take Action Project, keep in mind the difference between service and action: Service is direct and immediate; it changes something right now. Action, in contrast, gets at the root of issues to effect real and lasting change. Pages 68–71 of the girls' book further define service vs. action and offer up examples of how the two differ.

The stages that the girls will follow in their Take Action Planning Chart help ensure that they reach toward long-lasting action. The larger goal is for girls to develop thinking, planning, and engagement skills they can use all their lives. Some girls may even uncover issues they care deeply about and want to pursue further through other Girl Scout award projects.

Take Action Planning Chart

12 stages to a complete Take Action Project. Use the coaching tips here and the tools in the girls' book to guide girls to a meaningful experience and a significant impact on the community.

Take Action stages	To coach girls through this stage . . .	Tools	Page in girls' book
1. What are the issues?	**Raise awareness.** Expose them to a variety of issues that matter to girls and women—through news articles and firsthand research. Time permitting, suggest guest speakers or field trips so they hear about possible issues and actions firsthand.	• Surveys • Interviews • Brainstorm	86 89 82
2. Which issue are you choosing?	**Ask why "it" matters to them.** The motivation to stretch into uncharted territory and build new skills comes from truly caring about an issue.	• Community mapping • Brainstorm • Group decisions	91 82 61
3. What are possible solutions?	**Guide them to list and discuss possible actions for their chosen issue.** Encourage the girls to think about all the ways they could act on their chosen issue. Discuss the difference between "Service and Action." Zooming in on one aspect of an issue is often the best route to success.	• ID Issue	82
4. Which solution are you choosing?	**Discuss the scale and scope realistically.** Ask questions like, "How much time do you have for this? What is the greatest impact you can have with your resources?"	• Take Action statement • Case studies • Righteous indignation	94 72 79
5. How will you know when you've succeeded?	**Encourage the girls to envision the end result.** Suggest that they first imagine what good results would look like. Ask: What is your goal for the results of your effort? How would you capture that in one or two sentences? How will you define success? Assist girls to be as specific as possible.	• Vision	14–16, 94
6. Create a time line or calendar	**Offer some logistical guidance.** What is practical? Who can get where, when? How will the team adjust plans for the upcoming gatherings based on the Take Action plan? How can family and friends help?	• Time line	99

Take Action stages	To coach girls through this stage . . .	Tools	Page in girls' book
7. What resources will you need?	**Give permission to adjust plans.** Girls may realize they need to scale back their goal or change direction. Learning to "course correct" is a great leadership skill. Devising an alternate plan is a great opportunity for creative problem solving.	• Community mapping • Confidence	91 38
8. Who can help?	**Grow and diversify the network.** Building a network is a benefit of Girl Scouting that girls can carry with them all their lives. Encourage them to connect with peers interested in the same issues, adults who have access to resources and information, and organizations that have a stake in the issue. Encourage them to cultivate their network and use it to their benefit, even for college and job references.	• Community mapping • Networking • Confidence	91 65 38
9. Who will do what?	**Advise on cooperative decisions.** Get the team thinking about how to divvy up tasks. Maybe the girl who has time at night will do the online research and communicating. Encourage girls to think about taking on roles that will help them stretch and gain new skills and confidence. Perhaps a quiet girl wants to try publicity planning.	• Teamwork	62
10. Do!	**Keep the momentum going.** High school girls are busy. They may get discouraged if they don't find a way to see their plan through to completion. So encourage them if plans need to be altered. Cheer them on by reminding them of their visions. Ask other adults to support (but not direct) the girls.	• Voice • Publicity • Action Planning Chart	36 96 80
11. Evaluate	**Take time to assess.** Give girls time to think back: Why did they pick this issue and plan this action? What did they hope to achieve? How'd they do? Perhaps they want to make a "Next time . . ." list in their book. Encourage each girl to capture what this experience has meant for *her*.	• Evaluation	102
12. Reflect and Celebrate!	**Share insights.** Ask girls about lessons gained as they took action. How can they apply these to other areas of their lives? How might they use them on future projects? Encourage them to start an idea bank and to share it with peers. Encourage them to thank those who offered support (it keeps their networking going). Also encourage them to speak out, in big or small ways, about what they accomplished. It will inspire others!	• Appreciation • Reflection	100 104

Scheduling the Journey

ALL ROADS LEAD TO GIRLtopia!

Keep in mind that there's no "wrong way" to GIRLtopia. The sample sessions in this guide have girls doing their "Create It" and "Change It" projects little by little, with various GIRLtopia topics and "Guide It" opportunities mixed in. But the Seniors may want to complete their "Create It" first (Sessions 2–4 or longer) and then move on their "Change It" (Sessions 4–7 or longer), with "Guide-Its" all along they way. Alternately, the girls could focus Sessions 2–4 on GIRLtopia topics and "Guide-Its" before delving into their "Create It" or "Change It" projects. Let the girls choose their preferred path!

Assessing Time and Interest

Start the journey by asking the girls:

• *How much time do you want to spend "getting to GIRLtopia"?*

• *Do you want to earn the Girl Scout Senior Visionary Award?*

• *How big do you want to make your "Create It" projects?*

• *How big do you want to make your "Change It" projects?*

Create a team schedule together based on girls' responses.

This guide provides a sample schedule for an eight-session journey to GIRLtopia, with each session lasting about 90 minutes. You'll probably find that each sample session offers way more than your group of girls will cover! That's fine. The girls might really want to engage in one discussion or activity, but not another. So customize as you go.

Talk with the girls about how they want their journey to unfold. They might like to gather once a week over eight weeks. Or, if your schedules allow for flexibility, perhaps they'd prefer to experience the journey over a series of weekend retreats. Or maybe they want to stretch out the experience with gatherings and outings over six months or even a whole year. Girls may want to explore some of the journey's ideas and experiences on their own, gathering periodically to discuss their thoughts—or even setting up some online conversations.

As you and the girls create a schedule, be sure to reserve some time for just hanging out and enjoying the safe space and emotional connections so important to girls this age. That haven is part of what makes Girl Scouting unique.

Overview of the Girls' Book

The girls' book opens much like this guide, with an overview of what "Getting to GIRLtopia" looks like and the steps to earning the Girl Scout Senior Visionary Award. The pages that follow are filled with information, exercises, tips, tools, and reflections.

Familiarize yourself with the girls' book so you can easily reference it as needed. It's divided into four sections. **Why GIRLtopia** leads off, setting the stage for the journey. These fact-filled pages are followed by three main sections based on Girl Scouts' "three keys" to leadership:

Discovering YOUtopia invites girls to explore their ideal selves. They'll dive into conversations about leadership qualities, ethical decision-making, and develop the courage to express their true selves and have confidence in their skills.

Connecting Toward GIRLtopia invites girls to explore how they care about and team with others. They'll write a Girls' Bill of Rights, explore   cooperative decision-making and the dynamics of an "ideal group," and gain tips on networking. This section also includes subsections on celebrations and ceremonies and how they strengthen connections.

Taking Action on Your Vision provides the steps of a Take Action Project and all the tools girls need to implement one—from assessing issues and getting publicity to evaluating their project and celebrating.

MIXING IT UP

Girls needn't travel through the journey page by page, according to their book or your guide. In fact, the sample sessions in this guide often invite "mixing and matching" from the various sections of the girls' book. The book is the girls' to explore and add to as they wish.

Sample Sessions at a Glance

SESSION 1

GIRLtopia: What's It All About?

Girls learn about the choices involved in the GIRLtopia journey, including the Senior Visionary Award, begin to plan and schedule their journey, and

- gain an awareness of the need for a "GIRLtopia" and begin to express their visions for it
- explore their values
- build their understanding of visionary leadership
- start to plan their "Create It" projects and think about their "Guide It"

SESSION 2

What's on Girls' Minds?

Girls use decision-making skills to decide their approach to ceremonies, and

- promote team-building by determining how to act as an "ideal group"
- practice basic research skills as a way to explore community issues
- enjoy "Create It" time
- check in on the group's dynamics

SESSION 3

How's Our Community Doing for Girls?

Girls review the results of their surveys, and

- identify community needs through community mapping
- develop their own "Girls' Bill of Rights"
- continue their "Create It" projects

SESSION 4

Choosing to Take Action

Girls brainstorm to decide on the issue and focus of their Take Action Project(s), and

- practice making team decisions as they create a plan for taking action
- think about possible solutions to their issue

SESSION 5

What Would You Do?

Girls consider their values, and

- practice ethical decision-making
- plan their action projects
- assess their progress on shared goals
- have time for "Create It" and/or "Change It" projects

SESSION 6

What Do Leaders Sound Like?

Girls continue "Guide Its" (consider topics such as "Courage" and "Promise and Law"), and

- "Sound Off" on qualities of "leaders" and "nice girls"
- assess their team dynamics
- have time for "Create It" and/or "Change It" projects
- start planning a closing celebration

SESSION 7

How Will We Lead the Way?

Girls wrap up their "Create It" and "Change It" projects, and

- reflect on leadership values
- assess their team dynamics
- complete plans for their closing celebration

SESSION 8

Do I Inspire You?

Girls reflect on and evaluate their projects, and

- reflect on and evaluate their group dynamics
- reflect on leadership values (if not covered in Session 7)
- celebrate their success

Choice: It's All Up to the Girls

Girls in high school are juggling many demands—friendships, grades, sports, drama, dance, music, and other extracurricular activities. Many teens also have the added responsibilities of part-time jobs and/or helping out at home. And, of course, they are always craving opportunities to have fun and just hang out in a space where they feel accepted.

As a volunteer partnering with these busy and sometimes stressed-out girls, you'll want to find just the right balance between providing some much-needed structure and sitting back so that girls "get to GIRLtopia" in a way that reflects their needs and imaginations. This guide offers a wealth of information and a range of tips to aid in finding that balance.

As girls shape the journey and its schedule with you, be sure to brainstorm some "side trips" to inspire the girls to be truly visionary leaders. Consider for example:

- **Field trips:** Visits to regional sites and organizations related to the topics girls choose for their creative and Take Action projects. These might include art museums, galleries, and universities, especially art departments, women's centers or women's studies or human rights classes. As resources permit, so don't forget to include some time to check out the shops or the best place to sample new foods.

- **Networking:** Expand the girls' worldview by partnering with them to identify, and then visit with, adults and college students who can spark their imaginations. During a session on ethical decision-making, for example, perhaps invite women who have faced tough career decisions. The girls can take a role in sending invitations and confirming meeting arrangements and other details.

- **The Great Outdoors:** Check out your council's camp properties or the local park facilities, and head out for a weekend retreat. Giving girls a chance to get away from daily routines will really help them focus on creating their ideal world. You might even include a hike on which the girls share their ideas about the top-10 qualities of a leader. You could even invite other girls in your region who are also journeying to GIRLtopia.

- **Making Stuff:** Girls who like to make things—crafts, foods, inventions, videos, and other do-it-yourself projects—will enjoy sharing their talents with the team. Encourage the girls to share their favorite DIYs with each other—perhaps they can give each other what they make.

Family, Friends, and an Ever-Growing Circle

Girl Scout Seniors will likely have all kinds of ideas for their GIRLtopia journey, and they'll probably want some assistance in carrying them through. Just keep in mind that you don't have to be their only partner. Invite the girls' families and friends to get involved. And encourage the girls to think about other people they can tap. Mobilizing others is a valuable leadership skill.

The girls may even want to reach across the region to other Girl Scout Seniors journeying to GIRLtopia. Girls from rural areas might like to see what their urban or suburban peers are doing, and suburban girls might like to see what their urban and rural peers are up to. And when girls from various racial, ethnic, and socioeconomic groups can share ideas, even if just online, they all benefit. They're likely to think even bigger about their visions for GIRLtopia. Imagine the power of girls from an entire region showcasing their visions of an ideal world or hosting "Take Back the Night" action projects during the same week.

SHARING GIRLtopia

As the girls plan opening or closing events, ask if they want to invite their families and friends. It's a good way to share the ideal world they are envisioning and creating on this journey.

"What I like best about working with Girl Scout Seniors is that we can give them opportunities to try new things which might lead them to decisions about what they do or don't want to do for the rest of their lives."

—Jenni Glysson, Girl Scout volunteer and alumna, Ann Arbor, Michigan

YOU AND YOUR CREW OF GIRL SCOUT SENIORS

Throughout this journey, you and the girls will gain deeper knowledge of one another and the rich traditions of Girl Scouting. So take some time to understand the likes and needs of Senior-age girls, and then dip into some ceremonies and traditions of Girl Scouts and the "what and how" of creating quality Girl Scout experiences.

As you read about the long-lasting leadership benefits of Girl Scouting, think about your own perspective on leadership. Your interest and enthusiasm are sure to be a driving force for the Seniors.

Understanding Senior-Age Girls

Your ninth- and 10th-grade team members are going to expect you to really understand who they are. Keep in mind that girls this age:

Like to be included in setting rules,	*so take a back seat and let them make the rules and decisions whenever possible—as long as safety isn't a concern.*
Are beginning to clarify their own values,	*so give them room to not know every answer.*
Are beginning to promote individuality,	*so be sure to commend girls on their individual strengths, skills, and talents.*
Can sometimes be in a know-it-all phase,	*so be patient with them and provide lots of time for reflection/discussion in which they can think critically about their beliefs.*
Are developing stronger logic and problem-solving skills,	*so stand back as they organize and implement their own action plans, and let them find the resources they need.*

SAMPLING "GIRL WORLD"

Even if you are around girls a lot, teen culture is constantly changing. So consider spending some time:

- talking to girls in and out of Girl Scouts
- reading teen magazines
- watching movies/TV shows, visiting Web sites, and shopping in stores popular with teens

Then ask yourself:

- What issues do teens face today?
- How can I use my visit to "girl world" to expand and deepen my connection with teens?
- What did I find out that will make me a better guide on GIRLtopia?

For more tips on how to achieve the right balance between you and your crew of Seniors, check out this list:

Girls Like It When You . . .

Consider yourself an advisor or mentor and treat them as equal partners.

Understand that they need time to talk, unwind, and have fun together. This is a big part of why girls are in Girl Scouts.

Ask, "What do you hope to do on this journey? How do you want to spend time together?"

Help with the logistical details, paperwork, and legwork for projects and trips.

Trust them to get things done with minimal guidance.

Provide some structure.

Let them speak their minds. Try to let everyone have a voice, and encourage everyone to try on new roles in the security and comfort of the group.

Ask what rules they think they need for safety and what group agreements they need to be a good team.

Guide them by asking the right questions at the right times and help them act on their answers.

Focus on resolving problems with a positive attitude.

Try to stay up-to-date on the latest movies, music, celebrities, trends, and fashions. (But don't try to act like a teen—just be aware of teen culture.)

Let them know that you remember facing similar issues and have dealt with many of the same problems they are facing now.

Promote trust by letting them know that what is said in the group stays in the group—as long as safety is not an issue.

What + How: Creating a Quality Experience

It's not just what girls do, but how you engage them that creates a high-quality Girl Scout experience. All Girl Scout activities are built on three processes that make Girl Scouting unique from school and other extracurricular activities. When used together, these processes—Girl Led, Cooperative Learning, and Learning by Doing (also known as Experiential Learning)—ensure the quality and promote the fun and friendship so integral to Girl Scouting. Take some time to understand these processes and how to use them with Girl Scout Seniors.

Girl Led

"Girl led" is just what it sounds like—girls play an active part in figuring out the what, where, when, how, and why of their activities. So encourage them to lead the planning, decision-making, learning, and fun as much as possible. This ensures that girls are engaged in their learning and experience leadership opportunities as they prepare to become active participants in their local and global communities.

The "Guide It" suggestions throughout the journey are a great way for girls to take the lead. You can also:

• Engage the girls in scheduling how often, when, and where the team meets.

• Encourage them to "add on" trips and other activities that spark their imaginations.

• Have them identify topics that matter to them.

• Have them drive most of the planning, organizing, and implementation of their projects. (As the advisor, you will want to assist girls in thinking through the scale and scope of their projects and guide them toward realistic decisions based on their time and resources.)

Learning By Doing

Learning by Doing, also known as Experiential Learning, is a hands-on learning process that engages girls in continuous cycles of action and reflection that result in deeper understanding of concepts and mastery of practical skills. As they participate in meaningful activities and then reflect on them, girls get to explore their own questions, discover answers, gain new skills, and share ideas and observations with others. Throughout the process, it's important for girls to be able to connect their experiences to their lives and apply what they have learned to their future experiences.

So, for every experience girls have along the journey, encourage time for talking, sharing, reflecting, and applying their insights to new experiences in their lives. As girls lead each other in "Guide Its," they'll have a chance to practice the learning-by-doing approach themselves.

Cooperative Learning

Through cooperative learning, girls work together toward shared goals in an atmosphere of respect and collaboration that encourages the sharing of skills, knowledge, and learning. Working together in all-girl environments also encourages girls to feel powerful and emotionally and physically safe, and it allows them to experience a sense of belonging even in the most diverse groups. And through a commitment to teamwork, girls can see that an individual's success relies on the success of all.

Encourage Seniors to choose how they want to make decisions together on big and small matters.

TALK IS GOOD

Throughout the journey, encourage the girls to discuss what they are learning about themselves and leadership. Articulating their thoughts and feelings will consolidate their learning.

TOWARD AN IDEAL TEAM

Girls will also benefit from speaking openly and often about how they are functioning as a team. Sample Session 2 contains a "What's Our Ideal Group?" activity that the girls might find useful. Once they have described their ideal, they can use it periodically to reflect on where they are in achieving it.

Girl Scout Ceremonies and Traditions

E ven the briefest of ceremonies can take girls away from the everyday to think about hopes, intentions, commitments, and feelings. A ceremony marks a separation from whatever girls have just come from (school, work, dance class, math club), and creates the sense that what will happen now is special and important. So, find out how and when girls want ceremonies.

Girl Scout ceremonies can be as simple as gathering in a circle, lighting a candle, and sharing one hope—or reflecting together on one line of the Girl Scout Law. Or girls might read poems, play music, or sing songs. Invite them to create their own ways to mark their time together as special (some ideas are provided on pages 57–58 of their book).

SWAPS

Trading SWAPS ("Special Whatchamacallits Affectionately Pinned Somewhere") is a Girl Scout tradition for exchanging small keepsakes. It started long ago when Girl Scouts and Girl Guides from England first gathered for fun, song, and making new friends. Swaps are still a fun way to meet and promote friendship. Each swap offers a memory of a special event or a particular girl—it usually says something about a Girl Scout's group or highlights something special about where she lives. And it's simple; it could be made from donated or recycled goods.

CRAFTY TIP

On this journey, swaps can be issue-oriented. For example, a girl interested in improving child literacy rates could make a swap in the form of a tiny "book" by stapling together bits of paper.

Health, Safety and Well-Being

The emotional and physical safety and well-being of girls is of paramount importance in Girl Scouting. Look out for the safety of girls by following the Girl Scout resource Safety-Wise when planning all gatherings and trips, and

- checking into any additional guidelines your Girl Scout council might have based on local issues

- talking to girls and their families about special needs or concerns

- creating a safe and trusting emotional space for girls by partnering with them to make and stick to a team agreement

- reminding girls not to disclose their names, addresses, or contact information if they are interacting online

- calling on your council if you need additional expertise or referrals to community resources

Keep families in the loop, should important issues arise. Just let the girls know first. You can also talk with your council staff about available community resources (university centers, teen help counselors and groups) if specific expertise would be helpful.

Consider keeping an up-to-date list of the daytime phone numbers of all the girls' parents, guardians, or caregivers, should you need to reach them.

Welcoming Girls with Disabilities

Girl Scouting embraces girls with many different needs at all age levels, and is guided by a very specific and positive philosophy of inclusion that benefits all: Each girl is an equal and valued member of a group with typically developing peers. As an adult volunteer, you have the chance to improve the way society views girls with disabilities. One way to start is with language. Your words have a huge impact on the process of inclusion. People-First Language puts the person before the disability.

CONTACT INFO FOR YOUR GIRL SCOUT COUNCIL

Name: _____

_____

Can help with: _____

_____

_____

_____

Phone: _____

E-mail: _____

_____

SAY	INSTEAD OF
She has autism.	She's autistic.
She has an intellectual disability.	She's mentally retarded.
She has a learning disability.	The girl is learning-disabled.
She uses a wheelchair.	She is wheelchair-bound.
She has a disability.	She is handicapped.

Learn What a Girl Needs

Probably the most important thing you can do is to ask the girl or her parents or guardians what she needs to make her experience in Girl Scouts successful. If you are frank and accessible to the girl and her parents, it's likely they will respond in kind, creating a better experience for all. It's important for all girls to be rewarded based on their best efforts—not completion of a task. Give any girl the opportunity to do her best and she will. Sometimes that means changing a few rules or approaching an activity in a more creative way. Here are a few examples:

• Invite a girl to perform an activity after observing others doing it first.

• Ask the girls come up with ideas on how to adapt an activity.

Often what counts most is staying flexible and varying your approach. For a list of online resources, visit www.girlscouts.org and search on "disability resources."

Snacktopia

Food brings people together and offers an energy boost. Encourage the girls to decide on snack plans for gatherings. They might experiment with snack treats that are festive and uplifting: low-fat cheese on whole-wheat crackers, a pitcher of cold water with slices of orange floating in it, herbal iced tea, carrots with yogurt dip, hummus on pita. Think globally, and the options will be endless. The team can have fun trying to "snack smart" on the road to GIRLtopia.

Understanding the Journey's Leadership Benefits

Though filled with fun and friendship, GIRLtopia is designed to develop the skills and values teens need to be leaders in their own lives and as they grow.

Girl Scouts of the USA has identified 15 national outcomes, or benefits, of the New Girl Scout Leadership Experience. Activities in GIRLtopia are designed to enable 9th- and 10th-grade girls to achieve eight of these outcomes, as detailed in the chart on the next page. You can notice the "signs" of these benefits throughout the journey.

Each girl is different, so don't expect them all to exhibit the same signs to indicate what they are learning along the journey. What matters is that through GIRLtopia, girls build a firm foundation to be leaders—they discover important aspects of their identity, clarify their personal values, critically engage with the values of the wider society, and learn to communicate their needs to the wider world.

For definitions of the outcomes and the signs that Girl Scout Seniors are achieving them, see the chart on the next page or *Transforming Leadership: Focusing on Outcomes of the New Girl Scout Leadership Experience* (GSUSA, 2008). Keep in mind that the intended benefits to girls are the cumulative result of traveling through an entire journey—and everything else girls experience in Girl Scouting.

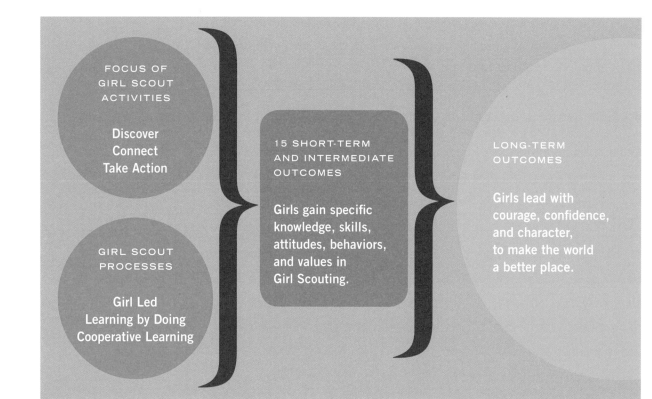

FOCUS OF GIRL SCOUT ACTIVITIES

**Discover
Connect
Take Action**

GIRL SCOUT PROCESSES

**Girl Led
Learning by Doing
Cooperative Learning**

15 SHORT-TERM AND INTERMEDIATE OUTCOMES

Girls gain specific knowledge, skills, attitudes, behaviors, and values in Girl Scouting.

LONG-TERM OUTCOMES

Girls lead with courage, confidence, and character, to make the world a better place.

NATIONAL LEADERSHIP OUTCOMES

	AT THE SENIOR LEVEL, girls...	SAMPLE "SIGN" When the outcome is achieved, girls might...	EXAMPLES of how the outcome plays out in this journey
DISCOVER — Girls develop a strong sense of self.	are better able to recognize and address personal and social barriers to reaching personal goals.	make connections between societal issues (e.g., prejudice based on gender or race) and their opportunities to achieve goals.	Girls learn about and reflect on the status of women and girls throughout the world.
Girls develop positive values.	strengthen their own and others' commitment to being socially, politically, and environmentally engaged citizens of their communities.	report increased positive attitudes of social responsibility and citizenship.	Girls envision a GIRLtopia, practice ethical decision-making, create a Girls' Bill of Rights, and Take Action to move the world closer to their ideal.
Girls develop critical thinking.	apply critical thinking skills to challenge stereotypes and biases in their lives and in society.	question assumptions behind inequities they encounter (e.g., female athletes earning less than male athletes).	Girls apply critical thinking throughout GIRLtopia.
CONNECT — Girls promote cooperation and team-building.	strengthen their abilities to build effective teams to accomplish shared goals.	identify specific strategies for building effective teams (e.g., paying attention to interests, strengths, team dynamics). demonstrate that they can reach consensus on common goals.	Girls assess their team dynamics— team-building that strives to reach an ideal.
Girls feel connected to their communities, locally and globally.	actively seek to bring people together in local and global networks.	give an example of organizing a local or global event that brought together diverse members of their communities.	Girls take on issues and meet others in the community in the process.
TAKE ACTION — Girls can identify community needs.	are more skilled in identifying their local or global communities' needs that they can realistically address.	identify community partners that can continue their project goals into the future.	Girls report considering multiple factors before deciding on the appropriateness of a project for their community (e.g., feasibility, balance of assets and needs, sustainable impact).
Girls educate and inspire others to act.	are better at inspiring and mobilizing others to become more engaged in community service and action.	shape messages to explain the importance of taking action on an issue they care about.	Girls shape their messages in their "Create It," "Guide It," and "Change It" projects.
Girls feel empowered to make a difference.	are better able to address challenges to their feeling of empowerment.	identify internal and/or external barriers to feeling empowered to create change.	In the GIRLtopia journey, girls learn of barriers to women and girls on a global level—and Take Action to break them down.

Your Perspective on Leadership

The Girl Scout Leadership philosophy—Discover, Connect, Take Action—implies that leadership happens "from the inside out." Girls discover their values and skills as leaders, and then connect with others to take action to better the world. This philosophy stresses the importance of working collaboratively with others to make things better for everyone. In Girl Scouts, a leader is not simply someone in a position of authority or someone who likes to be "in charge."

Before starting on this leadership journey, take some time to think about your own leadership philosophy. Your beliefs and values, and your attitude, will likely be a strong influence on the girls. Try the following reflection exercise, and revisit it throughout the journey.

DISCOVER

What do you believe about the status of women and girls in the world today? What are some of your personal values that shape these beliefs? (Keep in mind the statistics given on page 5 and check out the additional statistics given on page 9 of the girls' book.)

_____

_____

_____

_____

_____

_____

When you read the Girl Scout Law, what value speaks most to you? Why? How do you apply this value in your partnership with girls?

_____

_____

_____

_____

_____

_____

What impact does listening to girls and seeing their projects take shape have on your beliefs?

_____

_____

_____

_____

_____

_____

_____

_____

CONNECT

Consider how and when in your life you have experienced a great sense of belonging. Think of places or groups where you feel comfortable enough to say whatever is on your mind. How do people act to give you this feeling of true acceptance?

_____

_____

_____

_____

What aspects of those experiences, such as ways of interacting with others, can you encourage girls to try in their team?

_____

_____

_____

_____

TAKE ACTION

You are taking action as a volunteer in service to girls. Why? What motivates you to volunteer your time?

_____

_____

_____

_____

_____

_____

What impact do you hope to have on girls?

_____

_____

_____

_____

_____

_____

How can you coach girls to find Take Action Projects that truly matter to them and have an impact?

_____

_____

_____

_____

_____

_____

THE JOURNEY'S 8 SAMPLE SESSIONS

Before each gathering with the girls, you'll find it useful to read through the sample session or the revised session you have developed in partnership with them. Thinking about the session as a whole will help you concentrate on the potential impact each discussion and activity may have on the girls.

You and the girls will find it helpful to bring pens and scrap paper to each session. Many of the discussions and reflections call for girls to jot down ideas to share. Large sheets of newsprint and markers will also come in handy, as will scissors, tape, and sticky notes. Some sample sessions also note other simple materials specific to the suggested activities. There's no need for anything new, fancy, or expensive.

SAMPLE SESSION 1
GIRLtopia: What's It All About?

AT A GLANCE

Goal: Girls use positive values as the basis for thinking about how to make the world better for girls.

- Introduction to the Journey and the Senior Visionary Award
- Scheduling the Journey
- Why Do We Need "GIRLtopia"?
- Who's a Visionary?
- Shared Visions of GIRLtopia
- Envisioning GIRLtopia Through Art
- Signing Up for "Guide Its"

lead
respect
create
justice
imagine

Introduction to the Journey
and the Senior Visionary Award

Welcome everyone and invite them to welcome one another. If girls haven't met before, ask if they'd like to spend time getting acquainted. They might go around in a circle and say one thing they love doing—or answer fun questions they pose for one another. In large groups, encourage girls to meet someone new before the session ends.

For girls who want some more action, invite them to do an icebreaking game, such as this one, which can be prepared in advance or put together in a few minutes with the girls:

Tape one half of a set of paired words—such as sun/moon or salt/pepper—randomly on the girls' backs so they can see everyone else's word but not their own. The girls have to ask one another questions in order to find their "other half." Once they find her, the two "halves" talk together in order to discover one thing they have in common and one thing that is different about them. Once each pair of girls has chatted, each shares what it learned with the full group.

beauty

VISION

possible

paradise

power

dream

Scheduling the Journey

Summarize the GIRLtopia journey with the team. You could make points like this:

- *GIRLtopia is a journey to create an artistic vision of what an ideal world for girls looks like, and then move the world a step closer to that ideal through a Take Action Project.*

- *Along the way, you'll take turns guiding mini workshops so that we can explore various leadership topics related to GIRLtopia. Some topics might be: networking, making ethical decisions, having the courage to speak up for what we believe in, or any topics you come up with that relate to GIRLtopia.*

Engage girls in planning and scheduling. Consider these questions:

- How much time do they have overall for the journey: all year, six months, eight weeks?

- Do girls want to earn the Visionary Award (point out the steps on page 8 of their book) or do they just want to have interesting and fun times together as they journey toward GIRLtopia?

- How much time do they want to devote to their Create It projects as a group? How much time do they want to devote to it on their own?

- Does the idea of hosting an exhibit to showcase their artistic visions of GIRLtopia appeal to them or would they rather keep this aspect of the journey low-key?

- What kinds of "add-ons" might they like: outdoor activities, trips, time to hang out together?

- Based on the time girls can give to the journey, how much time do they want to give to their Change It projects?

Based on girls' ideas, guide the team to shape a general flow for the journey.

SENIOR VISIONARY AWARD

The Visionary Award is a prestigious award in Girl Scouting, so you might want to provide some context about it for the girls. Perhaps say:

The Visionary Award is about leading the way to make your world a better place. It's a real-life opportunity to make a positive difference for girls in your community. The award also honors your vision of an ideal world and what you have discovered about yourself and learned about leadership throughout the journey.

Juliette Gordon Low, in a French Farman plane with aviator Laurence Driggs in 1922. The two flew over Girl Scout headquarters in New York.

Why Do We Need GIRLtopia?

Open a discussion about why "GIRLtopia" is important and needed. You could, for example:

- Ask girls to consider the facts and questions in "Why GIRLtopia?" on pages 9–10 of their book. What else do girls know and think about related to girl issues—in their own lives or in the world?

- Invite discussion about the Oprah Winfrey quote on page 13 of their book: *"After the hundreds of stories I've heard of atrocities around the globe, I know that if you're a woman born in the United States, you're one of the luckiest women in the world. Take your good fortune and lift your life to its highest calling."*

- Point out the definitions and examples of utopias given in the girls' book and solicit further ideas from the girls.

- Ask girls about how envisioning an ideal community or society gives them the chance to discover the skills and strengths each of them could contribute to that society.

Who's a Visionary?

Ask the girls to break into pairs or small groups to create a Top-10 list of "visionary" qualities (page 17 in their book). Then bring the girls together in a circle and let each girl name at least one quality, value, or skill she has on her list, and one that she would like to develop during the journey.

Guide girls to think about their personal values and Girl Scout values. Get them talking about how these values will influence their visions and projects for GIRLtopia.

Begin by saying something like:

> Our values define what matters to us—and they are the lens through which we filter our ideas, opinions, and courses of action. In Girl Scouts, the Promise and Law define the values that shape our actions.

WHAT ABOUT BOYS?

Girls might wonder—what about boys? Invite the Seniors to look over page 10 of their book and notice the questions about how everyone can play a role in an ideal society for girls. What do girls think about this statement: In an ideal world for girls, the world will be more ideal for everyone.

If girls don't yet fully see why GIRLtopia is needed, don't worry—the journey invites them to explore why.

CRAFT-Y OPTION

Invite the girls to make a bookmark, card, or other keepsake listing their most important values.

Invite girls to spend a few minutes quietly looking over the Girl Scout Promise and Law. Then, guide a group discussion about those values. You might start by asking a few of the questions below and then just see where the girls take the conversation.

- *Which line in the Law means the most to each of you? Why?*

- *If you had to pick one line that you think is most important in your own family, what would it be? Why?*

- *What value in the Girl Scout Law is hardest for you to live by? Why?*

- *To what extent are your values influenced by the media?*

- *Think of people you consider to be leaders—in your own life and in the world. How do they live out one of the values represented in the Girl Scout Law?*

- *What kind of influence do the people you consider leaders have? Do they use their influence in positive ways? Explain.*

Relate the values discussion to GIRLtopia by asking:

- *What values would you like to see reflected in a GIRLtopia?*

- *How could that society not only meet your needs and celebrate your interests, but also meet and celebrate the needs and interests of other girls?*

Close the discussion by inviting girls to take some quiet time to reflect on what their personal Law might be. If there is time and interest, encourage girls to share (now or at a future gathering) their personal Laws with each other. Throughout the journey, invite girls to reflect on how their "Create It," "Guide It," or "Change It" projects reflect the values of their personal Laws.

TIPS FOR TALKING ABOUT VALUES*

- Discussing personal (or family) values may stir emotions—be sure the team's ground rules are maintained at all times.

- Emphasize that individuals differ, and there are no "right" or "wrong" answers.

- Body language says as much as words; stay nonjudgmental in all ways.

- If an argument over a value-related topic occurs, call a time-out for each side to clearly articulate its position.

- State clearly that you support everyone's right to express their values, whatever they may be.

- It is best not to share your own personal values (especially related to controversial topics). You can always say something like: *"Knowing my position may influence you, I'd rather help you figure you out your own beliefs."*

* Adapted from *Life Planning Education*, Advocates for Youth, Washington, D.C., www.advocatesforyouth.org

Shared Visions of GIRLtopia

To get the girls thinking in more detail about a society that truly respects and celebrates girls, say something like: *"Think about the ways in which the world is not perfect, specifically for girls. What problems or obstacles do girls face? In what way could the world be better just for girls?"* (Refer back to the earlier discussion, too.)

Ask for a girl to volunteer to create a master list of everyone's answers on a large sheet of paper. Then, take their ideas to a deeper level with this activity:

• Have each girl take a sheet of paper and write a one-sentence response to the phrase, *"In an ideal world, girls could _____"*

• Then have each girl pass her paper to the girl to her right, who will add her own sentence to the page—continuing the idea that the first girl started.

• The girls continue passing their papers to the right until each girl gets her original paper back.

• Ask the girls to read these GIRLtopia visions to the group.

Then ask the girls to reflect on these questions:

• *After hearing all of these GIRLtopia visions, what common ideas or suggestions do you notice?*

• *What surprises you in these visions? What about them interests you most?*

• *Think about the diversity of girls in the world. Could you create a GIRLtopia in which all girls would be happy? How or why not?*

Envisioning GIRLtopia Through Art

Guide the girls in brainstorming ideas for their creative visions of GIRLtopia:

- What type of artistic creation do they have in mind? What resources will they use?

- How much time do they want to spend on their projects? Will they work on them throughout the journey or only in the early sessions?

- Do they want to make individual projects or a group project? Let them know that individual projects could include poems, short stories, collages, paintings. Group projects could include a mural, a play, a video.

- Encourage girls to check out the inspiration section of their book.

When girls have reached their decisions, wrap up by reviewing any necessary logistics (supplies, advance prep) for the next gathering. If time permits, ask the girls to start thinking about how they might like to share their creative visions at the journey's end.

Signing Up for "Guide Its"

Close the gathering by inviting girls to flip through their books and identify topics, short activities, and "Think About It, Talk About It" sections that spark their interest (individually or in pairs). Then they can sign up to guide the group on that topic or activity at an upcoming meeting. Or girls might like to work together to create a "mini GIRLtopia" workshop or event for younger girls or peers outside this group. The choice is theirs. Notice that there are examples of possible "Guide Its" built into your sample sessions.

GIRLtopia "Guide It" Sign-Up Sheet

SESSION	DATE	NAME(S)	TOPIC AREA
2			
3			
4			
5			
6			
7			

Add-on experiences girls want to include in the journey?

_____

_____

_____

_____

_____

"In a perfect world . . .
girls' dreams could be limitless, and
no one would shoot them down."

—one girl's vision of GIRLtopia

SAMPLE SESSION 2
What's on Girls' Minds?

AT A GLANCE

Goal: Girls develop cooperation and teambuilding as they further develop their visions of GIRLtopia and begin thinking about possible Take Action Projects by planning to gather information.

- Opening Ceremony
- What's Our Ideal Group? (Girls might like to "Guide It")
- "Catch" the Dreams
- Skills for Taking Action: Surveying and Interviewing
- "Create It" Time
- Assessing Our Team Dynamics

MATERIALS

- Balls of yarn or string (for "'Catch' the Dreams")
- Scissors
- Tape or pushpins
- Strips of colored paper (or luggage tags)
- Paper clips
- Map of your community
- "Assessing Our Team Dynamics" list (created in Session 1)

Opening Ceremony (optional)

Encourage girls to think about how ceremonies might contribute to their sessions. You might prompt them by noting that a ceremony can be:

- a short experience that marks the start of a session and sets the time together as special and separate from the rest of the day

- a chance to connect with one another

Perhaps offer a few suggestions for an opening or closing ceremony:

- The girls might take a moment to think about their *ideal* leader—someone famous, a historical figure, or someone they know in real life. They would write a short letter or poem to that leader, explaining why she is someone they admire. At a future session, the girls could form a circle and one girl (or a few) would read her letter/poem to the group. Alternately, the girls could simply talk about why they admire their chosen leader. This sharing-of-leaders ceremony can be repeated throughout the journey, at the start or close of sessions.

- Or each girl might share a short poem she wrote, using at least four words from the "Assessing Our Team Dynamics" list of qualities selected for an ideal group environment (see "What's Our Ideal Group?" on the next page).

- Alternately, you might suggest that the girls create their own ceremony (such as a friendship circle or writing/singing their own song).

If opinions are mixed on what kind of ceremony to have—or whether to have ceremonies at all—perhaps ask the girls how they might make a group decision about ceremonies on this journey. If the girls choose not to have a ceremony, they can just dive into the activities of the session.

SENIOR VISIONARY AWARD

The Visionary Award is a prestigious award in Girl Scouting, so you might want to provide some context about it for the girls. Perhaps say:

The Visionary Award is about leading the way to make your world a better place. It's a real-life opportunity to make a positive difference for girls in your community. The award also honors your vision of an ideal world and what you have discovered about yourself and learned about leadership throughout the journey.

What's Our Ideal Group?

In this activity, girls define the ideal environment they want for their group, and practice negotiating common values as a team.

- Ask girls to break into small groups (three or four girls) to brainstorm the behaviors and attitudes they want in their group. Give each group strips of colored paper (or luggage tags) to write their ideas on.

- Explain that this is a chance for the girls to decide what they want their group to be like. For example, in an ideal group, how do they want to treat one another? What's the best way for girls to get along? How do they want to interact with you and other adults involved?

Reflection Questions for Group Discussion:

- *How does the environment you just described compare with other places or groups you belong to?*

- *Do you think our group's list for an ideal environment would be different if boys were a part of it? Why or why not?*

- *Can we say this list represents our group's values? (If helpful, come up with a definition for values, such as "personal beliefs that affect our attitudes and actions" or "what we would stand up for.")*

TIPS FOR LISTS

If girls are struggling with their lists, offer a few suggestions, such as: "no interrupting" or "the volunteer and girls make decisions together." Be sure the list includes "Having fun" and "Whenever possible, girls lead."

Also, explain to the girls that they can review the list at every session to see whether they are maintaining their ideal group environment. Keep in mind that this list will be used for the "Assessing Our Team Dynamics" experience in future sessions.

Skills for Taking Action: Surveying and Interviewing

"CATCH"
THE DREAMS

Make a life-size, but simplified, dream catcher—really a web of yarn—to "catch" all the girls' dreams for an ideal group. Start by handing out balls of string/yarn. As an entire group, construct the web (perhaps in a corner of the room) by securing its various threads to the walls or objects with tape or pushpins. Have girls hang their papers/tags in the web with paper clips.

Ask for a girl volunteer to write a list of all the ideas on a large sheet of paper.

As girls begin to think about possible Take Action Projects, they'll need some guidance about how to decide what would be a truly useful project for their community. It's important for them to get out into the community to talk to people and observe what's going on. Begin a discussion about the kinds of skills, such as surveying and interviewing, that the girls might need to accomplish this. Review with the girls the "survey" page in their book and emphasize that this is the kind of research needed to accomplish Step 1 on their Take Action Planning Chart. Ask questions like:

- *What can you learn by gathering information about what's on other girls' minds?*

- *What are some ways of asking girls how they would describe an ideal world?*

Drill down to the specific questions the girls might ask in their survey:

- *What kinds of things or places would you like to see more of to support and celebrate girls? What's your idea of a GIRLtopia?*

- *What would you like to change in your community to make it more ideal?*

- *How would you change it?*

- *What issues do you care most about?*

Remind girls that if GIRLtopia is to be a place that reflects the diverse interests, values, and needs of girls, then every girl needs to be heard.

Next, give girls time:

- to design their own basic survey and/or interview questions and commit to using them before the next gathering

- to make a list of people or groups they agree to approach with their surveys or interviews before the next session

Let girls know that at the next session, they will review what they've learned through their surveys and interviews in order to move closer to choosing a Take Action Project (the "Change It" step toward their Visionary Awards). Perhaps they can keep their eyes and ears alert for potential ideas. They might also like to check out the "Righteous Indignation" examples in their books.

"Create It" Time

Based on the girls' plans and interest, provide time for them to really dig in and concentrate on their artistic GIRLtopia visions. For example, if girls are making a video featuring various girls talking about their "ideal vision," they might use this time to plan—or even start filming—by interviewing each other. They could be writing poetry or a short play, or painting or making a collage. Girls doing more elaborate projects can use the time for planning and preparing.

As girls wrap up their creations for the day, ask them if they have decided whether they want to organize a gallery event or another type of viewing for friends, family, and/or the community. Talk, too, about reaching out to other groups of Girl Scout Seniors journeying to GIRLtopia. A regional exhibit of GIRLtopia visions could be quite exciting; it would be a tangible way for the girls, and others, to see what they want and need in their world.

REASSURE THE GIRLS

They don't need to do a major survey or be thinking about a huge Take Action Project. The idea is to get some new information and thinking going on as they consider various viewpoints. Perhaps they can even do their surveys in the course of a school day.

GOT MORE TIME?

Plan a field trip so girls can conduct a community survey. Decide which places or neighborhoods to focus on. Arrange to visit various schools, libraries, or other community locations. Malls can be a good place to conduct surveys. Remember to let girls set up the action plan.

Assessing Our Team Dynamics

Using their "ideal" list, girls evaluate their own group dynamics and practice negotiating common values as a team. Remind girls that this is an opportunity to *evaluate how they are doing at maintaining their own ideal group environment.* Invite girls to guide both the evaluation and recording processes.

- Hang the "Assessing Our Team Dynamics" list where everyone can see it. Let the girls decide on a ranking system (1 = not at all; 2 = some of the time; or smiley/frown faces). Then have girls rate their group environment based on each item on the list. (Be sure to label the girls' comments as being from Session 2, so they can keep track of their process/progress.)

Reflection Questions for Group Discussion:

- Was it easy or hard to reach a consensus as a group?

- Is there anything you want to change, any attitudes or behaviors, to make the group more like the ideal environment you want? Is there anything that we are not saying to each other that we need to be saying?

- Is being able to reach a consensus or negotiate with others an important leadership skill? Why or why not? If so, can you think of any real-life examples where a leader, either yourself or someone else, made a difference by using this skill?

ASSESSING OUR TEAM DYNAMICS								
SESSION	1	2	3	4	5	6	7	8
WE HAD FUN*								
THIS WAS A "NO INTERRUPTIONS ZONE"*								
OUR VOICES MADE A DIFFERENCE*								
WE MADE DECISIONS WITH OUR ADULT VOLUNTEER*								

1 = Not At All
2 = Some of the Time
3 = Mostly
4 = Lots!

*These are just sample ideas; the girls will use their own set of "ideals."

> ## "We've chosen the path to equality, don't let them turn us around."
>
> —Geraldine Ferraro, first woman nominated to run for vice president of the United States

Global Girls' Bill of Rights

Preamble/Statement of Purpose

We feel it is necessary to uphold girls' rights because:

....

....

....

We declare these rights to be self-evident, that all girls:

1. ....

2. ....

3. ....

4. ....

5. ....

6. ....

7. ....

8. ....

How's Our Community Doing for Girls?

AT A GLANCE

Goal: Girls identify community needs as they continue to develop their visions of GIRLtopia and make a Girls' Bill of Rights.

- Opening Ceremony (optional)
- Review of Survey Results
- How's Our Community Doing?
- Girls' Bill of Rights (perfect for a "Guide It")
- "Create It" Time

MATERIALS

- A map of your community
- Local phone books and newspapers

Opening Ceremony (optional)

If the girls chose to open the session with a ceremony, use the ideas they developed in the previous session or their own new ideas.

Review of Survey Results

Guide the girls to develop a list of their Top-Five issues from the data they collected in their surveys. Offer guidance or discussion prompts as needed, but let the girls lead the process of evaluating their data as much as possible. Ask questions like:

• *What issues seem really genuine to you and why?*

• *What issues do you think you could have an impact on?*

• *Which issues seem least important to you? Why?*

How's Our Community Doing?

To guide girls to learn basic community mapping skills, introduce the idea of mapping by saying something like: *Surveys and interviews are one way to build our understanding about ways we might take action. Community mapping is another way.*

• Display a community map or distribute copies of a community map.

• Share other relevant information about community resources: events calendars from the parks department calendars of events, youth services listings, the events sections of local newspapers. Note that most phone books provide listings of local resources and services, as do many Web sites.

• Get the girls thinking about the kinds of questions that will enable them to map their community assets, such as:

  Where do girls feel safe hanging out?

  Where do girls express themselves?

• Then brainstorm questions for mapping their community's deficiencies, such as:

  Are there safe and fun spots for teens to go to on weekend nights?

  Where is it unsafe for girls to hang out?

  Where can girls go for advice or assistance?

  Where would girls go for career information?

  What else do you need? Where can you find it? Anywhere?

- Mark with different color pins (or markers) the assets and deficiencies on your community map(s). Ask:

  > Looking at the deficiencies on our map, what can we identify as being needed by girls in our community?

- Make a list of these problem areas, or "hot spots," on a large piece of paper. Save this list and take it to the next session. Keep in mind that "hot spots" might not be places; they could be ideas, trends, or issues.

Let girls know that in the next session they will decide what Take Action Project(s) they will do. Suggest they flip through the examples and ideas in their book, especially the cases on pages 72–75 (but it's not homework! No test!). You might even ask the girls if there is anyone to invite to the next gathering who has expertise in taking action on a topic that interests them.

But if girls are ready, they could choose their project now—and come to Session 4 ready to plan!

Girls' Bill of Rights

(Perhaps a girl will want to "Guide It")

Ask the girls to mix it up by pairing up or forming small groups with those they don't usually spend time with. Have each team check out pages 54–55 in their book, where they are invited to create a Girls' Bill of Rights. When each team is ready, have all members form one large circle so that each smaller team can share with the group the right it feels is most important.

Reflection Questions for Group Discussion:

- To what length would you go to stand up for your rights? Who or what could stand in your way?

- Does passing a law ensure that individuals' rights will be secured? Why or why not?

- What ideas did we raise in doing this exercise that we might want to consider, along with the ideas we got from surveying and mapping for the Take Action Project?

Option: Go around the circle and ask each girl to name one adult and one friend she would go to for help if she felt her rights were being violated.

FROM VISION TO ACTION

Creative work often leads to great ideas. So ask the girls if anything bubbling up from their Create It projects has given them some ideas for taking action. After all, the goal is the same—a better world for girls.

"Create It" Time

Based on the girls' plans, provide time for them to work on their personal or group GIRLtopia art projects.

After wrapping up the art project time, ask the girls:

• *Does anyone have any general questions about the journey so far?*

• *How about ideas for interesting add-on activities related to our GIRLtopia theme? (Don't forget outdoor activities and meeting up with other Girl Scout Seniors.)*

Option:

If you have the time, invite girls to talk about Take Action Projects they know and admire. Here are two to share:

• Camille, 16, wanted to advocate for the gay and lesbian population in her community by working on related harassment issues in the local schools. So she asked her Girl Scout group to join her at a community youth organization called Outreach. Although she was nervous about sharing her idea at first, Camille and her sister Girl Scouts presented their approach to several school principals, and ended up counseling local school officials on how to handle harassment. Their efforts changed the climate in several schools.

• Teens Daria and Rayjean linked their Girl Scout group with an organization called Youth for Justice, after they learned that an old factory was being torn down and the land turned into a parking lot. The girls knew that their community needed a park to give children a place to play. Their advocacy efforts succeeded in stopping city planners *and* in involving the Parks Department. The title of the girls' advocacy campaign was "This is *Our* Community."

Ask girls to tell about any success stories they know of where girls have changed a community for the better.

In an ideal world for girls, the world will be more ideal for everyone.

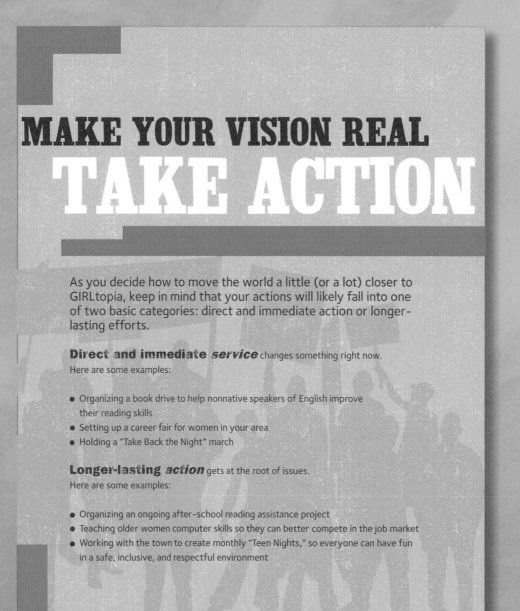

MAKE YOUR VISION REAL
TAKE ACTION

As you decide how to move the world a little (or a lot) closer to GIRLtopia, keep in mind that your actions will likely fall into one of two basic categories: direct and immediate action or longer-lasting efforts.

Direct and immediate *service* changes something right now. Here are some examples:

- Organizing a book drive to help nonnative speakers of English improve their reading skills
- Setting up a career fair for women in your area
- Holding a "Take Back the Night" march

Longer-lasting *action* gets at the root of issues. Here are some examples:

- Organizing an ongoing after-school reading assistance project
- Teaching older women computer skills so they can better compete in the job market
- Working with the town to create monthly "Teen Nights," so everyone can have fun in a safe, inclusive, and respectful environment

SAMPLE SESSION 4
Choosing to Take Action

AT A GLANCE

Goal: Girls identify an issue that impacts girls, brainstorm its solution, and plan for a Take Action Project that will move the world one step closer to their ideal.

- Opening Ceremony (optional)
- What Do You Want to Change?
- Casing Out the Possibilities
- "Change It" Time
- "Create It" Time

MATERIALS

- "Hot spot" list of issues from Community Mapping
- "Assessing Our Team Dynamics" list from Session 2

Opening Ceremony (optional)

Continue with the girls' ceremony ideas or invite them to connect with one another and share their hopes or anything they care about. They might do the ceremony they designed in the second session or any new ones they have thought of along the way.

What Do You Want to Change?

Girls decide on the issue/focus for their project.

Invite the girls to review and discuss what they have learned so far from their surveys and interviews and their "Hot Spot" list. They can also discuss the Take Action ideas and examples in GIRLtopia and ideas that have sprung up from their creative work. Remind them that they are now moving through Stages 2, 3, and 4 of their Take Action Planning Chart. Emphasize how these stages help ensure that their project will aim for long-lasting action, and not simply provide immediate service.

Ask the girls if they are interested in pursuing one project or several "mini team" projects.

- Do one or two ideas seem to be bubbling up the most? Ask girls if they are ready to decide and how they would like to go about deciding as a team.

- Do girls seem stuck and uninspired? Ask what they might like to do, know, or find out more about for inspiration. Engage them in planning how to go about getting more ideas so they can make a decision during the next session. Perhaps the "Casing It Out" exercise (next in this sample) will help. And, remind the girls that they don't have to do a Take Action Project, as long as they are OK with not earning the Visionary Award.

- Are the girls facing difficult logistical issues (such as transportation or schedules) that limit what they feel they can do? Encourage them to think creatively—there is always something they can do: letter campaigns, finding and inviting someone in who can "bring action" to where the girls meet, or a project that could occur during a school day. Keep the brainstorming going and a plausible, yet meaningful, idea will arise. If needed, use Session 5 to continue the thinking.

TAKE IT UP A NOTCH

Hold a debate or a town hall session where girls discuss, individually or in teams, why they think a particular issue is most important to take action on—and/or will have the most impact on girls in their community. This would be a good activity for a large group of girls from throughout your region to experience together. Encourage girls to do all the planning and run the show. It's a great "Guide It!"

MAKING A DECISION IN LARGE GROUPS

Have the girls break into smaller teams to decide which issue from the "Hot Spot" list they want to focus on for their Take Action Project.

• Invite girls to decide which issue they want to focus on, and to "make the case" for why their issue is most important.

• Ask each team to elect a spokesperson.

• Bring the full group back together and ask each group's spokesperson to "make their case."

• The girls can then decide on their top issue(s) *and* whether they will do a project as an entire group or break into smaller groups for several projects. Allow girls the opportunity to discuss and decide this for themselves; their project should reflect what they feel most strongly about. (If girls are having a tough time agreeing/deciding, ask them for suggestions for the best way to reach a consensus.)

WHAT IF . . .

girls choose an idea or issue that makes you or your community uncomfortable? This leadership journey is about girls feeling empowered to address issues that are important to *them; so try to coach them to find the aspects of problems that they can tackle appropriately!*

Girls sometimes need some guidance to consider an issue from various lenses so that they create a plan that will achieve the desired results amicably, without alienating any needed supporters. You can always seek feedback from the girls' families and your Girl Scout council if you and the girls need assistance thinking it through.

Casing Out the Possibilities
(a great "Guide It" opportunity)

Now that girls have picked an issue, they will think about all the possible solutions they could choose to act on, and try to zoom in on one solution that is practical—based on the time and resources they have. Your role here is to coach girls to think carefully about how they can have a meaningful impact. A clearly thought-out "small project" can have more impact then "big efforts" that are not clearly focused.

Invite girls to analyze and discuss the two case scenarios on pages 72–75 of their book. This will allow girls to critique plans and actions more thoroughly than they might on their own Take Action Project experiences. Discussing the cases (or creating their own for discussion) is a great "Guide It" opportunity for girls.

You (or the girls guiding the discussion) can ask:

- *What would have given these Take Action efforts more impact?*

- *What would have made them long-lasting?*

- *What ideas do these cases give you about your own plans?*

"Change It" Time

Invite girls to use some time now to plan their Take Action Projects, following that section of their books, and especially the planning chart on pages 80–81, to think through their projects—avoiding the case of the goody bags!

Encourage girls with a few points:

- *You'll know you have carefully focused your issue and solution if you can jot down—in a few sentences—what success will look like (Stage 5).*

- *Check out how you are progressing through the 12 stages of your Take Action Planning Chart! You are probably already up to Stage 5 or 6? Halfway done!*

Ask girls about logistics:

- *How can you break up what you want to do into some steps that you might be able to do during "the rest of your life?"*

- *Do you want some time in each upcoming session to devote to your project (even for just a check-in/progress report)?*

- *What other time do you anticipate you will need?*

- *Will you need to devote a few sessions just to working on the project or, if your project is bigger than initially thought, perhaps you want to add on a few sessions? Or do you want to adjust the overall journey schedule in another way?*

"Create It" Time

If girls are eager to work on their art projects, or are creating large art projects, let them use this time to continue working on them and making plans for sharing them. Ask:

- *Is there anything you want or need to do to organize the sharing of your art projects, such as posters or invitations, assistance with reserving a place or arranging refreshments?*

- *Who will volunteer to do what and when?* (Perhaps this can become a "Guide It" for interested girls!)

"The youth of the world should have standards and ideals in common."

—Juliette Gordon Low

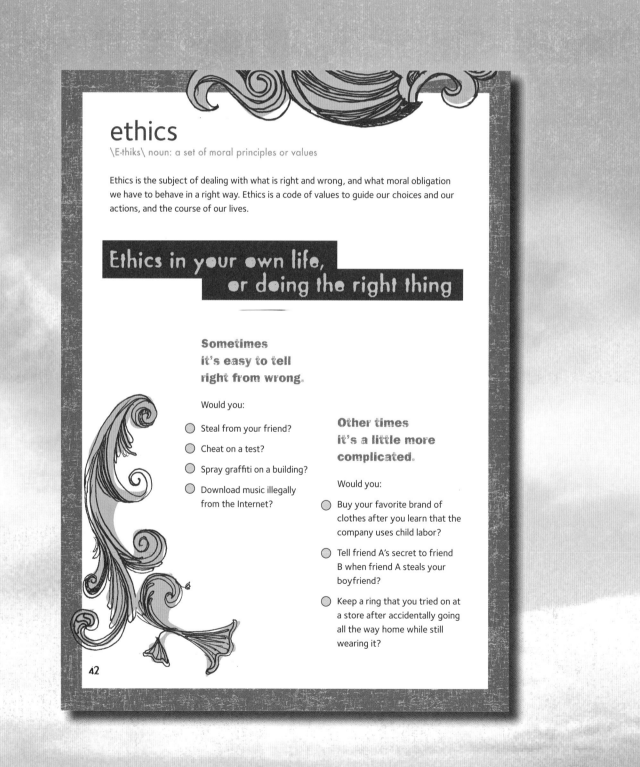

ethics

\E-thiks\ noun: a set of moral principles or values

Ethics is the subject of dealing with what is right and wrong, and what moral obligation we have to behave in a right way. Ethics is a code of values to guide our choices and our actions, and the course of our lives.

Ethics in your own life, or doing the right thing

Sometimes it's easy to tell right from wrong.

Would you:

- Steal from your friend?
- Cheat on a test?
- Spray graffiti on a building?
- Download music illegally from the Internet?

Other times it's a little more complicated.

Would you:

- Buy your favorite brand of clothes after you learn that the company uses child labor?
- Tell friend A's secret to friend B when friend A steals your boyfriend?
- Keep a ring that you tried on at a store after accidentally going all the way home while still wearing it?

SAMPLE SESSION 5
What Would You Do?

AT A GLANCE

Goal: Girls practice ethical decision-making and continue to develop their critical thinking skills as they plan, carry out, and assess their creative and/or Take Action Projects.

- **Opening Ceremony** (optional)
- **Take Action Time Update Conversation** (as needed, if girls devote time in each session to their projects)
- **"Create It" or "Change It" Time**
- **Ethical Decision-Making**

PLANNING THE UPCOMING SESSIONS

Arrange Sessions 5–7 so that girls can complete their "Create It" and "Change It" projects. Make a little time to discuss their progress and next steps. Depending on the plans and timing, the group may want to continue making a little time to engage in the various activities and discussion topics in their book. For example, the Ethical Decision-Making exercise on page 65 of this guide is another "Guide It" opportunity for girls.

Opening Ceremony (optional)

Wherever they gather, girls may enjoy conducting a brief opening or closing ceremony of their choice, marking their progress getting to GIRLtopia.

Take Action Project Update Conversation

As the project unfolds, engage girls in discussing their progress and feelings. Try asking questions like:

- *While doing this project did you meet anyone you didn't know before? What have you learned from that person? How is your network expanding through this project?*

- *What kind of impact do you think the project is having? Why?*

- *Have you encountered any unexpected challenges? How are you working around them?*

- *What do you need help with? Whom can you ask?*

- *Are you on track with your time frame? Do you need to make some adjustments?*

- *Which "stage" on the Take Action Planning Chart do you think is most important? Why?*

- *If you were starting over, would you do anything differently?*

Give girls plenty of encouragement for their efforts. Remind them that just trying makes them successful!

Ethical Decision-Making

(great "Guide It" opportunity; also good for a retreat)

Referring to the ethics section that starts on page 44 of the girls' book, start a discussion about the various ways to make ethical decisions. Ask the girls to give examples from their own lives of when the various ethical "tests" applied to a decision they made on their own.

Then, have girls think about ethical dilemmas they face in their own lives:

- Ask them to write one dilemma on an index card and then put their cards in a hat.

- Each girl then picks an index card from the hat and creates a short skit to perform about that ethical dilemma.

- Encourage the girls to think deeply, saying: *Be sure to play the story out as far as it can go. Ask yourself, What would happen then? And then? And then?*

Then, get a discussion going by asking:

- *What kinds of ethical decisions do individuals have to make that affect their local communities?*

- *What kinds of ethical decisions do individuals have to make that affect the global community?*

- *Do you think leaders have a responsibility when it comes to making ethical decisions? Why or why not?*

Then move the discussion to some broader reflection questions:

- *Do you think your personal values are reflected in your community's values? If so, how and where? If not, why not?*

- *Let's think about leaders for a moment and what values they represent. Think of a leader—someone famous or someone you know—and name the value you think she most stands for. What actions or decisions has that leader made that showed you what she stands for?*

ETHICS OPTION

Divide the girls into small groups and invite each group to pick an example from the case studies about ethical decision-making on pages 49–51 of their book. Ask each group to discuss a case and talk about what they would do. They might even play out the cases further, asking what would happen next.

"**I'm quite assertive.** If I didn't speak the way I do, I wouldn't have been seen as a leader."

—Kim Campbell, former Primer Minister of Canada

SAMPLE SESSION 6
What Do Leaders Sound Like?

AT A GLANCE

Goal: Girls refine their Take Action and/or creative GIRLtopia projects and explore leadership.

- **Opening Ceremony** (optional)
- **"Change It/Create It" Time** (as needed, if girls devote time in each session to their projects)
- **"Guide It" Time**

- **Sound Off: Thinking Outside the Box** (another "Guide It" opportunity)
- **Assessing Our Team Dynamics**
- **Planning a Closing Celebration**

PLANNING THE UPCOMING SESSIONS

If the team will be ending the GIRLtopia journey after Session 8, you'll want to engage the girls now in planning some closing celebrations and firming up any last aspects of their "Create It" and "Change It" projects, including opportunities to showcase their artistic visions.

Opening Ceremony (optional)

If girls are enjoying having ceremonies, continue to invite them to perform a ceremony of their choice that connects them to one another and the journey.

"Guide It" Time

Have all interested girls (especially those going for the Visionary Award) had a chance to conduct a "Guide It" discussion or activity for the group? Make time now and in Session 7 for girls who still need a turn. There's "Courage," starting on page 34 of the girls' book, "The Promise and Law" on page 51, and much more for girls to use or build upon for a "Guide It."

The following "Sound Off" activity is a wonderful active exercise. It's followed by a discussion that gets the girls thinking through all they have learned as leaders on the road to GIRLtopia. You can even invite a girl to "Guide It."

Sound Off: Thinking Outside the Box

Ask the girls to brainstorm qualities that make "a nice girl" and qualities that make "a leader" and write them on separate index cards. Put the cards in a bag or bowl and then:

• Have each girl pick a card and tape it to her shirt.

• With a roll of masking tape, make a large symbolic box on the floor. Girls wearing a quality that represents "nice girls" stand inside the box, and girls wearing a quality that represents "leaders" stand outside the box.

• Have girls compare the qualities in the "nice girl" box with the qualities in the "leader" box and reflect on the similarities and differences.

• Time permitting, have the girls pick new cards from the bowl/bag and do another round.

Reflection Questions for Discussion:

• *Is it possible to be a leader and a "nice girl" at the same time? Why or why not?*

• *What female leaders—world, local, personal—do you admire? Why?*

Share with the girls the quotes on the following page and invite them to discuss how they feel about them.

"I don't have a traditionally female way of speaking . . . . I'm quite assertive. If I didn't speak the way I do, I wouldn't have been seen as a leader. But my way of speaking may have grated on people who were not used to hearing it from a woman. It was the right way for a leader to speak, but it wasn't the right way for a woman to speak. It goes against type."

—Kim Campbell, former Primer Minister of Canada,
quoted in the Harvard Business Review, September 2007, page 65

"I used to speak more softly, with a higher pitch. Sometimes my vocal cadences went up instead of down. I realized that these mannerisms lack the sense of authority. I strengthened my voice. The pitch has dropped . . . . I have stopped trying to be everyone's friend. Leadership is not synonymous with socializing."

—Nien-hwa Cheng, symphony conductor,
quoted in the Harvard Business Review, September 2007, page 66

Assessing Our Team Dynamics

Continue guiding the girls (or ask them to guide one another!) in a discussion of their group dynamics, evaluating their efforts and reflecting on how they have created common values as a team. Use the list established during Session 2 (see page 49) as the basis for the discussion.

Reflection Questions for Discussion:

• *What have you learned about forming a group that strives toward an ideal environment for girls?*

• *Have you been able to apply this group process to other groups or clubs? Why or why not?*

• *What is the best part of how our group has interacted?*

• *What could we have improved?*

Planning a Closing Celebration

Invite the girls to look at the "Celebrate" page in their book (page 108) and chat about ideas for closing the journey together. Girls might like to keep it simple—a little party or retreat or outing for the team. Or, they might like to open it up, inviting community members they have met during the Take Action Project, other Girl Scouts, and their families and friends. Encourage girls to plan the kind of closing celebration that interests them. Ask those who are earning the Visionary Award if they would like to receive it as part of the celebration.

Also, are girls planning some type of "gallery" viewing for their creative projects? Do they want to combine that with the closing celebration? Ask:

• *Who should be invited (for enjoyment and to increase awareness of your issues)?*

• *How will you explain the purpose of the gallery to guests?*

• *What tasks need to be divvied up?*

• *Do any girls still looking to do a "Guide It" want to take on a special role?*

"Vision without action is merely a dream.
Action without vision just passes the time.
Vision with action can change the world."

—Joel Barker, futurist, filmmaker, and author, from "The Power of Vision"

SAMPLE SESSION 7

How Will We Lead the Way?

AT A GLANCE

Goal: Girls wrap up their "Create It" and/or "Change It" projects and explore leadership.

- **Opening Ceremony** (optional)
- **Take Action Project Discussion**
- **Exploring Leadership** (a "Guide It!" opportunity)
- **Assessing Our Team Dynamics**
- **Planning the Closing Celebration**

PLANNING THE UPCOMING SESSIONS

Depending on the scale and scope of the girls' "Create It" and "Change It" projects, the team may still be wrapping them up. If so, you can incorporate the "Thinking About Leadership" exercise (suggested in this session) into Session 8. Reflecting on women's leadership will make a fine closing to the journey—and a springboard to whatever Girl Scout Seniors decide to do next.

Notice, too, that "reflecting and evaluating" ideas are provided in Sample Session 8. Girls can begin those here if they are ready. This is an especially good idea if they plan to have festivities and guests at the closing.

Opening Ceremony (optional)

If girls are enjoying taking time to reflect about being on this Girl Scout journey together, encourage them to continue their short opening or closing ceremonies. They can use a tradition they started in an earlier session—or try something new.

Take Action Project Discussion

Start a discussion with the girls about how they will wrap up their "Change It" efforts. Any unforeseen challenges to work around? How will they thank supporters? Encourage them to check out the "appreciation" section that begins on page 100 in their book.

Invite the girls to consider exactly what they are learning as they progress through the 12 stages of Taking Action. Ask questions like:

- *How do the 12 stages make this project different from other efforts to help out that you have been involved in before?*

- *How could you apply these stages of action to other areas of your life?*

- *Have you checked off all the stages? What's left?*

- *Have you uncovered another Take Action Project you might like to pursue— perhaps related to earning other Girl Scout awards?*

Exploring Leadership

(a "Guide It" opportunity)

These exercises would be perfect for a little retreat or outing the team might add on before ending the journey—or even for the closing. Be sure to allow time for girls to reflect on their ideas after the experience.

To guide girls to define leadership for themselves, invite them to choose one of the following two activities in their book:

- "Ode to a Leader" on page 32, in which the girls read their letters aloud to the group

- "Leadership Talk Show" on page 33, in which girls can ham it up a bit while covering some serious points.

GOT MORE TIME?

Ask the girls to make a list of local women they consider leaders— personal or public—and then invite one or more to speak to the group. The girls may even want to organize a Speaker Series at a local library or school. The speakers can likely help the girls explore career options, too. Just encourage the girls to brainstorm career-related questions for the speakers, including ones about their education and any obstacles they may have faced.

Assessing Our Team Dynamics

Girls evaluate their group dynamics and negotiate common team values, using their "How Are We Doing" list, as in previous sessions. Continue with reflection questions as well:

- *Is there anything you want to change, any attitudes or behaviors, to make our group more like the ideal environment you want it to be?*

- *How can a list like this—a list of shared values—help to bring the members of a community together?*

- *In what other ways, or areas of your life, can you apply this code of behaviors or values?*

Planning the Closing Ceremony

Before the girls head out, take a few minutes to finalize plans for the "end of journey" celebration.

"There are two ways of spreading light:
to be the candle or the mirror that reflects it."

—Edith Wharton

INSPIRATION

SAMPLE SESSION 8
Do I Inspire You?

AT A GLANCE

Goal: Girls share their GIRLtopia projects and celebrate the success of their Take Action Projects.

- Reflection and Evaluation
- Sharing the Creative Projects
- Award Ceremony and Celebration

Reflection and Evaluation

Gather the girls in a circle and guide them in reflecting on their personal leadership experience during the journey. Go around the circle and ask each girl to share something she has gained from her journey with the group. Perhaps girls would like to share something from their "Reflection" (pages 104–105 in their book).

Optional: Invite the girls to autograph one another's books with thoughts about what they have learned together on the road to GIRLtopia.

Invite girls to look at "Evaluation" (page 102–103 in their book) and start a discussion. (Large groups might break into small teams for this.) Ask:

• *What is most important to you about what you accomplished on your "Change It" project?*

• *What have you learned that you will carry with you the next time you Take Action?*

Sharing the Creative Projects

If girls have not had a chance to showcase their art projects, take time for each girl or team to present her creative project and the statement it makes about GIRLtopia.

Award Ceremony and Celebration

Conduct whatever ceremony or celebration the girls planned. If you are presenting the Senior Visionary Award, consider telling each girl something you learned from her, something you appreciate about her, or a way in which she personally inspired you. And then celebrate! You and your crew of Girl Scout Seniors created GIRLtopia!

Now, Take Some Time for Yourself

When the celebrating ends, take some time to think about your own journey to GIRLtopia. Look back at the leadership reflection on page 28. Has your view of the status of women and girls in the world changed at all through this journey? What impact do you think you've had on the Seniors?

Has GIRLtopia changed you in any way? What about your vision for an ideal world for girls? What are you doing to get the world one step closer to that ideal?